HOLLY

SURVIVING THE

Dick Clique

A GIRL'S GUIDE TO SURVIVING THE MALE DOMINATED CORPORATE WORLD

Table of Contents

Acknowledgments

First off I have to thank and acknowledge my family. They are my foundation and support system. My partner, Abraham Elhiany, and my fabulously funny daughter, Stella. My parents, Lee and Ralph Caplan, who watched me grow, mature, and find my way through my career. My sister, Allyson Caplan, and my niece, Amanda Bingham, for reading every chapter and every rewrite.

And, of course, I need to thank so many wonderful women that either helped me with topics, guidance, and feedback, or have been loyal friends for years. Elaine Angelo, Hilary Stec, Jean Laino, Suzy Hastedt, Mary Griffitts, Tara Martin, Moira Fitzgerald Ryan, Josie Beck, Christa Allan, Holly Clegg, Ally Cavanagh, Jeni Laux, Lisa Robbins, and Deb Gelman.

I also have fantastic non-dicks to thank—Steve Tomminello, Dave Delia, Robert Hornak, Todd Paulette, Bronk Harms, Todd Galski, Michael DeCarlo, Ryan Griffitts, Chris Warner—for standing by my side and being supportive.

I do have to thank the Dick Clique, too. How else would this shit get written?

Disclaimer

This is a work of creative nonfiction. The events are portrayed to the best of Holly Caplan's memory. While all the stories in this book are true, **some names and identifying details have been changed to protect the privacy of the people involved.**

Preface

The purpose of this guide is to help women navigate their corporate careers in a male-dominated world. I share my experience and the wisdom earned through failures and successes, through moments of humiliation and years of camaraderie, to encourage women who may feel at times lost in the perplexing thicket of the dick clique.

In 1994 I was a recent college graduate and could not wait to attack the world. I was so naïvely excited about my life, career, and future. I thought I knew so much and had so much life experience, when in reality I was as green as it gets.

Let's go back to the 70s and 80s first, though. . . . I was raised in Baton Rouge, Louisiana—a great town to grow up in. Back then it had a population of around 400,000 with great food and lots of culture (which it still has). As for inside my own home, I was very sheltered and protected. My parents were extra cautious with me, perhaps because I was the firstborn. I didn't really have to think for myself. They solved any problems or issues, filtered my circle of friends, and sent me to a small, private school. I grew up in a bubble. It was a very safe space. Luckily, as a kid I didn't have any negative experiences and I was surrounded by good people. I didn't know of anything really bad. My parents taught me a lot, but that was all good, too. They taught me to be respectful, kind, and compliant. This was my foundation. I thought this was how I was supposed to be and that everyone else would behave the same way. Pretty basic, right?

However, as I became an adult I encountered new challenges outside of my safe Baton Rouge bubble. If I was faced with a dis-agreement or discomfort, I didn't know how to handle it. Bottom line, I had to learn on my own to confront conflict. My method was genius—I became flustered and would just shut down, which I'm still known to do upon occasion.

I chose to stay in the BR bubble going into college as I started Louisiana State University at seventeen years of age. This led to six years of undergrad. Yes, six years. Here is a recap of those six years: I drank too much. Smoked too much. Shacked up too much. And, most certainly, I did not study enough. I didn't take life seriously. I couldn't have given a shit about my grades. All the kids around me had goals and knew what they wanted to do. They were worried about their careers, report cards, and test results. As for me . . . *meh*. I did not have the internal drive to be a high achiever. I was still in my safe bubble and in denial that I would ever grow up.

Surprisingly, this all changed once I graduated. Totally changed. (Yes, parents reading this, this can happen.) I knew I had to kick it into overdrive because I now had to take care of myself, and that started with me. I was in charge of my own survival and success.

One thing I did know—I was determined to live in a big city, be independent, successful, and have a great career. I couldn't imagine my life any other way. For this I needed money, and I surely did not have the brains or attention span for medical school or law school, so sales it was.

The big city I chose was Houston, Texas. Only a four-hour drive from Baton Rouge, and certainly big and glossy enough. So, I did what everyone did in the early 90s when looking for a job—I looked in the newspaper's want ads (yes, millenials, that was a thing). Somehow through my newspaper want-ad search I landed my first corporate job in Houston. Hallelujah! I was legit. I lived in a large city and had an outside sales job. This first job was selling long-distance phone service to businesses. Yeah, I know, glamorous. I thought I was the shit. I learned how to make cold calls, telemarketing calls, and overall just be damn aggressive. I got beat up daily by prospects on the phone or in person. But I didn't care. I thought it was the best job ever. In my first year I made $38,000. At twenty-four years old, I thought I was rolling in the money.

Little did I know that that job would be the stepping stone into sales roles with different medical device companies and ultimately into a long-term medical device sales career. Even though I knew that the medical device industry was cutthroat and male dominated, I had no idea what I was getting into. Recruiters and colleagues repeatedly warned me how rough it was, but I went in blindly and hoped for the best. I started as a sales rep, became a sales trainer, and then ultimately earned a management position. Throughout these successes and promotions, I became more engaged with more men.

The higher you go, the more men there are. It took me years to realize this, and I was simply not prepared.

Preparation is the purpose of this guide. I am aware that plenty of you reading this have similar backgrounds, or share similar dreams and aspirations. I want to prepare those of you who are entering your career or are in the throes of your own success. The more successful you become, the more you will find yourself side by side with the opposite sex. You will share space with them in what has been traditionally considered male territory. I want to coach you for what is coming your way. I want you to be ready for those moments when you're shrugging your shoulders wondering, *What do I do with this situation?* So, Ladies, this is for you.

My Dick Is Bigger Than Yours

T he true translation of the phrase, "My dick is bigger than yours," is "I'm establishing my rank." What I learned rather quickly in the corporate world is that men have to prove that they are the best and the smartest in the room. There is a constant need to outdo each other. Most men, save a few, in the corporate world function under this premise. This behavior baffled me for a while. I didn't understand it because as a woman I did not function in the same manner. In my mind, I was in the boardroom to attend a meeting and work as a team to address whatever was on the agenda. So, when I saw this "big dick" thing, it was hard for me to comprehend, and it made me uncomfortable, especially being the only woman in the room. So, in an effort to understand it and survive in it, I sat back and observed how they interacted. In doing so, I was able to break down their behaviors into *how they do it* and *why they do it.*

My Personal Analysis of HOW:

1. They will insert themselves into a conversation in which they do not contribute, but need to be heard.

2. They will brownnose the highest level of management in the room.

3. They will shame a colleague who is either present or not present.

4. They will find weakness in others and use it against them.

5. They will exhibit a constant need to one-up each other.

By this point, the penis measuring stick is out and the contest has begun. I liken this behavior to marking their territory, or ensuring that they are on the top of the food chain and clarifying to one another where they rank in their world as well.

As a woman entering this environment, you will find this behavior appalling. Their constant need to outdo each other is exhausting. I wanted to gauge a better understanding of *why* this behavior is necessary and *why* it is accepted.

My Personal Analysis of WHY:

1. Survival—They need to constantly be recognized within their group of peers. It is a function of the male ego to feed the need to be relevant, even in the most irrelevant, meaningless ways.

2. Acceptance—This behavior has been occurring for a long time, is accepted as the norm, and is rarely challenged. In my personal experience, it is rewarded in their own circles and tolerated by the human resources department.

I know what I speak of here may be considered harsh and raw, but it's real. After years of being exposed to this environment, it had an impact on me. So much so, that I started to engage in the same behaviors. Unconsciously at first. If I was going to succeed, make a name for myself, and make money, I had to survive in the dick clique. I became argumentative, confrontational, and started to mark my territory just like the rest. The sad thing is that this behavior bled into my personal life. I started to treat everyone and everything around me in the same manner. I became increasingly impatient, competitive, and identified the worst instead of the best in people. I developed a level of self-righteousness. My then-husband said I had begun to act "like a dude." He was right. Even my sentences started with "Dude." I started drinking like a guy and gave up almost every basic emotion. When other people were emotional or showed weakness, I didn't understand how they could let themselves fall apart. I had lost any softness, compassion, understanding, and patience. It was true. I had become unforgiving, cutthroat, and insensitive. I went through years where I could not cry or feel emotion.

I had become a DICK.

1

Bars and Boobs

You Don't Have to Be the "Cool Girl"

Okay, I really wasn't sure if I should bring up this point, but a friend of mine's husband thought it was relevant to the guide. And he's right. As much as I really don't want to discuss strip clubs in the corporate world, as it seems so trite, it is a reality, so here we go.

You will be invited out to drink with the boys after business events. This is not uncommon, and can certainly be done harmlessly, but be sure to do it carefully. You will also be invited to strip clubs with those same boys. This is where you, as a woman, can cross a line and end up in a rather uncomfortable situation. I have engaged in both of these events.

Bars

While it might sound great to go out for a cocktail or two to bond with colleagues, we all know we can lose our best judgment. But sometimes we do this anyway because we want to develop relationships with our coworkers on a different level. Spending time with the guys and cutting loose can be fun. You can commiserate on professional issues, get to know each other personally, hear about their families, etc. But, really, I did it for acceptance. I did it because I wanted them to accept me as one of their own. I wanted to be seen as one of the "guys" who could hang, shoot tequila, stay out late, and do it again the next night. I wanted to be the "cool girl." I wanted the guys to trust me and know that I was on their team. That I wasn't going to be some bitchy, needy, high-maintenance chick that would only hold them back from their male activities. So I made an effort to be in the dick clique and show them that I could do this too. That I could drink Johnnie Walker, smoke cigars, act like a fool, and still get up and put my lipstick and heels on the next day and make a presentation at a meeting.

Example:

Oh, so many examples here. Where to begin? My memories of drinking with work buddies are really all blurry—pun intended. My bad choices included drinking too much, staying out too late, smoking cigarettes and cigars. But what I remember most clearly is the suffering that comes after a night of drinking. I think I threw up in pretty much every hotel at which I had a sales meeting or training from 1994 to 2010. I suffered through many a meeting with cold sweats, nausea, bad breath, and wishing I had never been born. This led to a miserable flight home, and ultimately an unhappy spouse who didn't understand or excuse my exhaustion when I returned after a sales trip. Unfortunately, over the years I have seen people take drinking and bad choices a step further and really end up suffering when they are ultimately fired in the end.

When it comes to drinking irresponsibly at corporate functions, I have witnessed a bodily injury that required hospitalization, passing out in bathrooms, leaving a bar in a wheelchair, sharing nude selfies, and, of course, the good ole hookup. I've seen sales reps sent home from meetings because of these behaviors, never to return to the organization.

The drinking experience that stands out the most was after a rather intense sales meeting and everyone was ready to cut loose. We all went out in groups for lavish dinners and then agreed to go to a new hot spot. Upon entering this hot spot, one of my colleagues told me we had a "table." This should have been my first clue that this was going nowhere good. Naïve me, I didn't even know what that meant. I grew up in Louisiana and Texas, where we stood around and drank. We didn't need a table, or "table service." Next thing I knew, scantily clad women showed up with sparklers and bottles of champagne. One of them asked me for my credit card as it would be needed to proceed with our evening. I went to my manager, who was with us at the time, and told him they wanted my credit card. I asked for his, as the the manager was to pick up the tab . . . this was a company rule. Let's just say he told me to use mine. He was my superior, so I took his direction and handed my card over.

The evening turned into a blurry, sparkly, drunk dancing, lushy evening. One of my colleagues ended up puking and passing out in a bathroom. Another couldn't fly home the next day—she had to check herself into a hospital because she was so dehydrated. This is the very short version. Not to mention my spouse was pissed off because he didn't see why I needed to stay out until 3 a.m. Oh, and my bill at 3 a.m. was $6000. Yep.

Months later I got a call from our HR department wanting to know why this was expensed. I thought I had covered everyone who attended that evening with the $6000 charge. Come to find out, several of the other managers in attendance all had large charges. Altogether, that evening's expenses totaled over $20,000. We all got warning letters from HR that became a permanent record in our files. And as for my manager? Despite the fact that he told us to use our cards, fully knowing company policy, he would not take ownership of the evening. He went into self-preservation mode and plead innocent to HR. He sold us out and proceeded to go back to business as usual, unscathed.

I saw what his core was made of. I saw how quickly he would turn his back on his own team to keep himself safe. This forever changed my view of this person.

Lesson on Bars:

When it comes to impressing your colleagues, you don't have to be the cool girl. Although it is a human need to be accepted, don't feel pressured to do so. They will like you, or not like you, for who you are. We are all grown-ups, aren't we? And if they don't think you are cool, tell them to go back to high school.

I also encourage you to watch yourself not only for your career's sake but for all of the obvious safety reasons as well. Just be careful. Use the buddy system and common sense.

Rules on Bars:

1. Be in charge of your own destiny and leave the event early. Do not become a victim of the evening's events. (I did not make this choice enough.)

2. If something seems sketchy, it probably is (see $6000 charge).

3. Do not exit alone with a male, unless he is your brother. (Common sense.)

4. Do not drink too much. You will feel like ass the next day, and any drunken behavior will instigate conversation about you from the clique.

Drinking and carousing can be career killers and will always follow you. Trust me. It is a very small world.

Boobs

Yes, this happens and it happens often. Men are still men. Fathers, husbands, brothers, friends, it doesn't matter. A lot of men, not all, but a lot of them enjoy frequenting strip clubs when they are away from home. This was a little eye-opening for me, as I thought in modern days that men wouldn't really feel the need to attend. However, there is something that draws men to being surrounded by naked women. You will be invited to attend by the dick clique. The decision to accept will be yours.

Example:

As a twenty-something I so badly wanted to relate to the men on my sales team, that in the 90s I did go to a strip club with them during a regional sales meeting. I thought it would give me a chance to be the cool girl and understand this male bonding by lap dance. I was actually able to witness several lap dances—some involving my male colleagues and some involving other male patrons. I had never seen one before. What I quickly realized is that there was no dancing involved. The lap dance is really just a dry humping session. Really, that's it. Just a woman, in a G-string (no bottomless at this fine establishment), grinding away on a fully clothed man. These dry humping sessions—let's call it what it is—were going on all around me, in big, soft, fluffy chairs in the middle of the room, or in a dark corner at a small table. I studied the men on the receiving end of these dry humping sessions, because I wanted to understand their reaction to all of this, as admittedly I was in shock. I found that each man, chair to chair, corner to corner, shared the same reaction. I like to refer to it as "masturbation face." Heads tilted back, eyes half closed, mouths dropped open with their tongues resting gently at the bottom of their mouths. All of these men looked like they were about to orgasm at any moment. It was like I had invaded the personal bedrooms of these men during their most private moments . . . or what should have been private moments. But you know what? No one seemed to care what the others were doing in this dark, smoke-filled room of soft light and big boobs. These men did not acknowledge each other. It was like a silent code. "Don't look at me, and I won't look at you." It was an unspoken understanding they had between them. From a male perspective, I'm assuming they got some fulfillment out of these lap dances, or dry humping. I'm not sure. But I saw desperation, emptiness, and sadness. Especially as the dry humper dismounted her dry humpee with cash in hand, ready to traipse off to her next customer.

Later that same evening, while drinking at a corner table with my male colleagues, I had a heated argument with a stripper about which one of us was really a businesswoman. Ironically "businesswoman" was her theme that evening, and we were both in suits. Mine just provided more coverage. My conversation with the "business" stripper was based on what we each do for money. She argued that she sells her product and gets paid for it just like I do—despite the fact that she had no formal schooling, professional training, award-winning rankings, nor had ever given a presentation in a boardroom. I found this somewhat unsettling. Maybe it's because I'm still kind of worried she won that argument.

The aftermath of this event wasn't just my new cultural knowledge of male behavior in these establishments. It was the cover-up of the whole event. My district manager gave instructions the next day that were twofold. The first was how to expense our drinks from the previous evening. Each of us had picked up a tab at some point. The receipts proactively and creatively read "Joe's Ice House." How smart of the strip joint to embed such a cover to assist business patrons so our expense reports would not raise a flag with the accounting department. Whew. The second instruction was, "Do not tell my wife. She will kill me." All of us knew his wife because we had met at group events. She was a really nice person. I wasn't comfortable, but now I had committed to the secret. Any of these activities would or should get someone fired in the current environment—going to a strip club, expensing it, and lying about it.

Lesson on Strip Clubs:

The lesson here is not complicated at all. It is very simple. Short and sweet. It isn't funny, it's not a bonding experience, it isn't professionally ethical, and if you really want to look at a pair of breasts, go home and look in the mirror.

Rule on Strip Clubs:

1. Don't go.

2

Odd Woman Out

Being Excluded

Rarely will you find yourself in the inner circle of the dick clique. I can't tell you how many times I have been left out of it. If you are in a group setting, they will walk ahead of you, ignore you, and most likely not invite you to whatever pre-dinner or post-dinner events are taking place. I have been in bars in which I attended with them and then they left me behind without telling me where they were going next. It's like being walked out on—scratch that, it *is* being walked out on. They will also talk about you behind your back and make fun of you to their colleagues. This behavior is no secret, although perhaps they think it is. An interesting point is that the more women I talk to who are also in the corporate world, the more I find out that we share this experience of being excluded by the dick clique.

Example of Exclusion:

Over ten years ago I was at a physicians' conference on the East Coast. While at our company booth in the vendor area, I was speaking with a doctor about one of our devices and technology. While I was asking this doctor certain probing questions, a product director named Paul (we'll call him) walked right up and took over. I had not asked him to enter the conversation, nor did I need him in the discussion. His dick was in full force. I had seen this before. Paul would interject himself and take over the conversation. I just stepped away. It wasn't worth fighting for, as I wasn't a Paul fan, anyway.

A couple of hours later during a coffee break, I was returning to the booth and I came across Paul and some of his buddies who also worked for our organization. I overheard Paul talking about me behind my back, and the word used was *clueless*. It stung a bit. I filed it in my memory and decided to deal with him one on one. I called him later that evening, and requested he meet me in the bar for a conversation. I told him that I heard his "clueless" comment and wanted to know why he said that. I honestly don't even remember his response because he was so rattled that I busted him in the first place. He stammered and backpedaled his way into a jumbled mess of words. After this conversation, my working relationship with Paul was never the same. Not that it was great in the first place. Oh, and just so you know, Paul and his buddies were all fired within the following six months. Not due to me. Just being themselves.

Lesson on Exclusion:

Know that members of the dick clique find strength in their pack. It is much easier for them to exclude a female colleague than involve her. I have found this in multiple situations from sales team to sales team. This exclusionary behavior is not confined to one organization or to one specific group of men. It is a culture. I don't know if it is because they really consciously or subconsciously think women are the lesser sex or if they are flat bothered by the fact that a woman is capable of doing the job. It sounds awfully archaic, but there has got to be a science to this. (I'll leave that to the experts.)

Rules on Exclusion:

1. If you are faced with being excluded in a social situation by the dick clique, know that this has nothing to do with you. They are going to stick with their pack. The pack is their comfort zone.

2. Be confident and speak up if you feel that you have been slighted, discredited, or walked out on. Call them out on it.

3

Dicks on Display

Do Not Trust Anyone

As a woman, I want to trust people. I want to know that they inherently care about me as I do them. Although this will be your natural inclination in your career, be wary. You will find a few you can trust, but they are rare. The sad thing is that not being able to trust anyone will break a part of you. You can feel isolated, and you constantly have to watch your back. After years of being in circles of men and witnessing the beer drinking, fist bumping, and bloviating, one would think you were in a fraternity house. I thought it was just me, a woman, who would be excluded, talked about, and made fun of. I thought a very tight circle of men would trust and protect each other to the end. They seemed so impenetrable, tight, and secure. Not necessarily so.

Example on Trust:

After a sales meeting ended—I mean, the sales reps had literally just walked out of the door—my manager and his colleague cornered me in our meeting room. Let's call them Eric and David. Eric and

David wanted to get my opinion on how I thought the reps performed during our meeting as they each had to role-play how to sell a product. Each rep had to get in front of the room and pitch our new product. The whole thing was a shit show. The reps were so nervous about this exercise. They knew Eric and David would be judging and criticizing, and not in a healthy or productive way. Ultimately, in this post-meeting meeting, Eric and David told me how awful the role-plays were. They made fun of a few people, and questioned their true abilities in the field (this was also a punch at me as these reps were under me).

They then asked me who on the team was my go-to person was for knowledge on this device. I mentioned the person, who happened to be one of their buddies. Let's call him Brian. When I said I was going to Brian for help with the product, it quickly became clear that these two men were not on his side. They rolled their eyes and sighed. Eric and David quickly told me to not consult Brian again (supposedly their friend) and to only contact them if I needed assistance in product-related matters. They leaned back in their chairs, looked down their noses, and described Brian as an idiot and loose cannon. To me, this whole situation was a power play, unsurprising considering the egos of Eric and David. I was being ganged up on as was Brian (unbeknownst to him). This was a painful conversation because I had so much respect for Brian, and thought they did too. One would think they would have handled it in a different way, perhaps professionally, especially because he was their friend. It hurt to know how they really felt about him. I also now knew that if they were capable of having conversations like this about Brian, they were certainly capable of having them about me. My trust, any that I had left, dissolved. I hate to say this, but this is a prime example of the dick clique. And this will sound sick, but I was so accustomed to this environment that I accepted it, and just walked away from this meeting pissed.

Lesson on Trust:

My lesson was hard learned as I could not figure out the best way to handle these situations . . . for years. The example with Eric and David is just one of many.

Eric and David got so much satisfaction from shaming the sales reps and Brian in order to reinforce their own perceived rank. Looking back I wish I would have defended the innocent more. I wish I would have pushed back on their words. I would have challenged them. I would have told them I don't respect how they are approaching this situation and then left the room. Sounds great in retrospect, doesn't it? I didn't have the balls though. I felt it was safer to just keep quiet and deal with it. I know what you're thinking . . . contact HR! Quite frankly, I'm not sure HR knows how to handle these situations. Unfortunately for me, when I did bring similar issues to HR, they would consult the dick, and then the dick would bully me more. It became an unstoppable cycle.

Rules on Trust:

1. Lead by example and protect those you can trust. Let your colleagues know they can trust you and live up to your own words. You will earn respect and create solid relationships (I did not do enough of this; I shut down).

2. If your gut tells you that you cannot trust someone, your gut is probably right. Follow that instinct. Keep your distance, and keep your communication professional.

3. Do your best to not let this part of the dick clique get you down. Rise above it and know their antics are purely for their own ranking maneuvers. Know your real value and appreciate it.

4

Kleenex and the Clique

Crying

S ad to say, but as a woman, you have to keep your composure. Whatever you say or do will be used against you at some point, and this includes crying. Crying can be viewed as manipulative or weak. That said, I have been on both sides of this situation. I have been the crier, and have been cried to. Men see a woman crying in the workplace as weak or crazy, and will hold it against her (I know, not a shock). They do not know how to handle it. I have spoken to them about this, and it makes them very uncomfortable. They have equated it to having a breakup conversation with a female, but the female doesn't want the breakup. Awkward. Uncomfortable and regrettable. Just as well, I have had women cry to me about work situations. This is dangerous, even with me as a woman, because, depending on the context, I can figure out the motive of the tears and the true goal of the conversation.

Examples:

Being the Crier

I had a big falling out with a sales manager I reported to years ago. Let's just say it involved my credibility and honesty coming into question about a large sales deal. In the middle of closing this deal, it began to unravel. The reason for the collapse fell on our shoulders, not the hospital. When we explained to the hospital where we had screwed up, the shit hit the fan. The administrators and physicians at the hospital were very upset. Thankfully, the deal closed ultimately, but the screwup was projected on me. My superior took no responsibility. It turned into a nightmare as all involved parties from our organization were summoned to HR to give their individual accounts. I felt like I was on trial, trying to plead my case. I was in fear of losing my job and was being bullied throughout this situation. I had to have HR step in more than once. I suffered sleepless nights, chest pains, and a negative impact on my homelife.

Although the work situation was resolved, my relationship with this man, the sales manager, was never the same, by which I should not have been surprised. A year after the incident, he and I were on the phone, and this topic came up. In our conversation, my voice cracked and I told him how hard it was to get through those days. Unplanned, I found myself in tears. The hurt I experienced from our debacle the year before was still raw and unresolved. I felt sad, humiliated, and frustrated all at the same time. Although it was cathartic for me to speak about it, and a little embarrassing due to the tears, the conversation did not result in any type of self-awareness for his part in the episode. It was like being emotional with a brick wall. He made no apology or effort to make amends. I didn't expect an apology because of my tears, but I had hoped to witness some human element in him through our conversation. I didn't find it.

Lesson on Being the Crier:

Ugh. Crying was not a good move. I should have known better. I should have politely hung up the phone and had a good cry on my own. To this day I feel embarrassed that I let those tears flow. Don't expect those who have hurt or slighted you to have awareness of the impact of their actions. You can't change anyone. The only thing you can change is how you handle yourself.

Being Cried To

I once had a rep who wanted a promotion after a year of employment with us. She was not my hire; however, she shared with me that the person who did hire her said she would be promoted within six months. She thought her time was overdue. She was at a year, and "What were we going to do for her?" There was a level of entitlement I did not understand. I was not the one who promised her anything, nor did her behavior or performance warrant a promotion. She called me at 6:30 p.m. on a Thursday to have this drooling, sloppy conversation. At first I tried to be patient and play therapist, but realized it was falling on deaf ears. She didn't really hear me as she was so wrapped up in her own emotions and motivations. At the end of the phone call, this person was no closer to getting a promotion, and in my mind her career path had now taken a sharp turn in the opposite direction.

Lesson on Being Cried To:

When it comes to a professional situation, approach it professionally regardless if you are dealing with a man or woman. Don't start with emotion. Think about things methodically and have a plan before you call your manager about something like this. In retrospect, she should have documented all of her accomplishments, emailed them to me, and scheduled a call to discuss the issue. This way, we could have focused on her career path and set realistic expectations. This was also a lesson for me as a manager, and that lesson was: I should have ended the phone call immediately, and rescheduled it for a time when she wasn't so upset.

Overall, I do not advise or like women crying in the workplace. If you have a situation that you find frustrating or emotional, know where it is coming from and work through it before having a conversation in the workplace. I understand there are some days when we are more fragile than others. I understand there are some days with overwhelming circumstances. I understand that sometimes crying is unavoidable, as I've been there. Just try to be prepared before engaging in what you believe could be a teary situation.

Rules on Crying:

1. Do not waste your tears on a member of the dick clique. They do not know how to handle it.

2. Do not use crying to manipulate the other party.

3. Be prepared and think through what could be a potentially teary or emotional situation before you have a conversation.

4. If you are caught off guard, and crying occurs, excuse and collect yourself. Return to the conversation when you are ready.

5

Predatorial Pricks

Bullying

I have talked a lot about our survival as women, but I have not addressed male survival—it frequently takes the form of bullying. I'm aware that it has been a common thread throughout this guide, but I want to address it head on. Dick clique bullying comes in different forms and is expressed in different ways. It can appear as shaming, being passive-aggressive, or just a direct kick in the balls. For the dick clique, this is their means of survival. As I mentioned in the first section, it is accepted and encouraged behavior among male groups. I found it incredibly disrespectful and frustrating. The downside of this for me was that I got so used to it I didn't see it anymore and accepted it as normal behavior. I learned that being disrespected and disrespecting others was okay, as long as you came out on top.

I have so many examples—some short, some long. I'll provide you with those that stand out the most for me as they had a strong impact and stuck with me the longest.

23

Example:

I was managing a sales team and had an opening for a new sales rep in my region. My manager at the time wanted to join me for a round of interviews, as he was the one who ultimately needed to sign off on our next hire for the territory. This manager was loved, hated, and feared all at the same time. He had been with our organization for years. He was very smart, yet was known for being a bully. The human resources department had even approached him over the years about complaints people had made, but of course he was not challenged and there was no change in his behavior. Bullying had become his M.O. and was accepted and tolerated.

Two interviews from our days together really stood out for me. The first is when we were interviewing an older man who had years of experience with a large medical device company. Upon meeting him, you could see he was a kind person with a gentler approach. My manager saw this as weakness and immediately honed in on it. Like a predator. I felt like I was watching a kill on *Mutual of Omaha's Wild Kingdom*. After reviewing his resume, this is how the dialogue went:

Manager: "So, you think you can do this job?"

Candidate: "Yes, of course."

Manager: "I don't believe you." Shoulder shrug and bottom lip pushed out.

Candidate: "Really? Why don't you think I could do this job?"

Manager: "You aren't strong enough. I don't think you could handle it or are qualified."

Candidate: "You don't even know me, but you are making these statements."

Manager: "Yeah, because that is what I see."

Candidate: "Well, are you telling me I'm wasting my time?"

Manager: "Yes, because I'm not going to hire you, so yeah, you are wasting your time." Leaning back in his seat with arms crossed.

Candidate: "So, are you saying I should leave?" Awkward pause.

Manager: "If you want to, that's up to you." Another dismissive shoulder shrug.

The candidate was clearly flustered and uncomfortable. He wasn't sure how to handle this conversation. He picked up his items and walked out. That was it. That afternoon I received an email from him telling me how awful the interview was and that he could not believe he was spoken to that way. He said my manager was unprofessional and could not imagine how anyone could work for him. He was right. I was just as shaken as he was.

We had another interview the next day that went in a similar fashion. It was the same thing: weakness identified, *Wild Kingdom*, walk out, email in my in-box.

Guess what I did? Nothing. Not a damn thing. After both of these horrible interviews, my manager stated what idiots those people were and made additional condescending remarks. I laughed it off with him. I thought I was part of the dick clique and that these matters didn't matter. I needed to be cool and accepted by him so that my job was secure. How sick was that?

In addition to that shortcoming, both of the emails I received from the candidates stopped with me. I did not send them to HR or bring up how terrible my manager had acted to anyone who could have made a difference. I swept both scenarios and their aftermath under the rug. Guess what that did? Enabled more bad behavior and made me feel like an asshole.

Lessons on Bullying:

I wish I would have gone with my gut. Common theme here, right? I wish I would have addressed my manager after the first interview and told him that his approach was unprofessional and rude. I also wish I would have written both of the candidates back, apologizing for their experience, and then forwarded their emails to human resources. I feel like I sold these two people out, because I set up these interviews and made them vulnerable to the Wild Kingdom experience. I let them be torn open, eaten, and then disposed of. I did nothing to stop it or make apologies. This did nothing for my self-respect, and I'm sure those two people still don't respect me.

Rules on Bullying:

1. Confront the bully that made you uncomfortable. Speak up.

2. Don't let the bully influence you. Practice respect. For yourself and those around you.

3. Report it to HR and tell them what transpired. Provide details and documentation. I'm not promising it will be completely addressed, but at least it will be in their file.

6

Do Not Become a DICK

Stay True to Yourself

You will get used to the culture of the dick clique and find yourself thinking the same way they do. Certain behaviors like bullying and being entitled are not okay, and you will lose sight of this. All of the chest pounding and entitlement is bullshit. It is easy to become a dick after being exposed for a certain period of time.

Example:

At a national sales meeting some years back, I found myself acting like a complete asshole to a respected, very kind colleague of mine. Ironically, her name was Holly, too, but spelled with an "-ie." She was a super sharp girl and was great at her job. While we were at an awards banquet earlier that week, a sales rep from my team had earned rep of the year. While receiving his award on a stage in front of the whole company of two-hundred-fifty people, he thanked me, Holly, as his manager. A couple of days later, I was in a conversation with the other Hollie, and she was telling me how flattered she was that this winning sales rep thanked HER for his achievements. My blood started to boil, my heart raced, and I thought, *No way am I going to let her take credit for this.* Right in front of other people, I looked at her and said, "Hollie, you know that is my rep, and he was thanking me, right?" I was so determined to make sure that I was recognized and appreciated in some capacity, I was willing to make a complete ass out of myself. Come to find out, she was speaking of a different situation completely. It was not related at all to the awards banquet. I was so embarrassed and ashamed of myself. I mulled over this conversation for about an hour, wondering if I would seem like a puss if I called her to apologize and recognize my regression. The dick clique ego in me initially thought no. Why should I do something to make another person feel better about an uncomfortable situation? I went with my gut, ate crow, and called her that evening and apologized for being such a dick. To this day, I still hope she forgives me.

Lesson on Not Becoming a Dick:

Do not emulate those around you. It is easy to adapt to their culture, especially when you want to succeed and survive it; however, adopting their survival technique is not the way. It is just a place where they have been for a long time. Be aware of how your actions impact others. Stay empathetic. Welcome others' success. Don't make yourself the center of the world, because you are not (no one is).

Rules on Not Becoming a Dick:

1. Do not emulate those around you. Copying bad behavior will not get you anywhere good.

2. Do not attack someone to spare your own ego.

3. Do not let your ego drive unhealthy behavior. It will breed anger, resentment, and hostility in your daily life.

7

Fuckable Factor

Protect Your Brand

As women, we are taught to use our sexuality from a very young age. As young girls, all of the fairy tales tell us to do so. Look at Cinderella or Snow White as a starting point. We are taught that if you are beautiful and young you will eventually get what you want and marry the man of your dreams. With the assistance of small mice, birds, and dwarves, of course. This still occurs in cartoons or in story lines in the preteen shows on television. Although these stories don't necessarily result in marriage as in olden days, they do still teach the standard expectation of a female. We have been taught that we need to be fuckable to have worth. And, need I even mention social media driving how women use sexuality? How many profile pics have you seen of a woman showing her cleavage in a revealing outfit, or in a bathing suit? This has become society's way of branding, and unfortunately has translated into the real world. Your brand becomes your reality. My ultimate message in this section is to protect your brand, and help you make the right choices, but not without sharing my mistakes and others' first.

Example on Wardrobe:

My second real job in the corporate world was as a sales representative with a medical/pharmaceutical company. It was a rather large company, and my first national meeting consisted of about three hundred people in my division alone. What I remember the most, outside of initially feeling a bit lost, was how good-looking everyone was. Each rep, male or female, was dressed impeccably and was devastatingly attractive. This was also a fun environment, especially as a single twenty-something. We worked hard during the day, and partied at night. At night there were always big functions for us that included dinner and lots of alcohol. Here is where my mistake came in, using my sexuality to seek attention. I wanted to keep up with this crowd. I needed to stand out. So, I thought I had to hooch it up and try to look hot. At one such particular event, I decided to wear a very short black skirt with black go-go boots. I strolled through that event feeling sexy and empowered. I really thought I was something.

I was trying so hard to get attention, it backfired. The next day, one of my female colleagues came up to me and said we needed to talk. She was older than me and had been at the company much longer, so I knew I would respect whatever it was she had to say. She told me that my outfit from the night before was inappropriate, not a professional choice for my environment, and that it had the dick clique talking about me, but not in a good way. This was so embarrassing. I was so humiliated. What the hell was I thinking? I didn't want this lapse in judgment to be my brand. I felt vulnerable and stupid. So, I attempted to redeem myself in the coming events. I presented myself as more conservative and professional, which really wasn't a problem. I just had to realize that people would respect me and like me without having to use my sexuality to get attention.

But wait . . . I made this mistake AGAIN a few years later. I attended an awards banquet and chose to wear a rather hot, fitted, red dress I had purchased a few years prior. The thing is, I had gained about fifteen pounds upon entering my thirties. The dress wasn't just "fitted" anymore—it looked more like it was struggling. But for some dumb reason, I chose to Spanx it up and make the damn thing work. It didn't. I remember walking to the banquet from my hotel room thinking, *Oh, shit. I can't breathe. Oh, shit. How am I gonna sit in this thing? Oh, shit. Why didn't I choose a more appropriate dress?* Apparently I was again the topic of conversation amongst the dick clique, and not in a good way. Not only did my female colleagues tell me this, but my male counterparts were very direct by asking if I had breast implants put in, or by telling me that my boobs looked great. I was like, "Nope. I'm just fat and made a bad choice."

Lesson on Wardrobe:

My point with this example is that using your sexuality to get attention by wearing a skimpy or revealing outfit at a corporate event is not the way to go. It might feel like fun, and you may be beautiful in it, but save it for a date or nightclub. As a result of my actions in the previous example, I lost some of my self-respect and the respect of others. I was pretty upset with myself because I knew better. I was taught better. As for my colleagues, thankfully, my mistakes disappeared into the past. Other women who came into the organization after me made the same mistakes and the focus was on them. I was able to redeem myself, not only for those around me, but for me.

Rules on Wardrobe:

1. Do not dress to flaunt your sexuality around your coworkers. Save it for your husband or boyfriend. Spare yourself from attracting the wrong attention.

2. If you question a dress or outfit for a business event, trust your gut and choose a safer option.

3. Spanx does not solve all problems.

Wearing sexy clothing isn't the only way to use your sexuality. There is also flirting. I'm a terrible flirt, so I don't have much experience in this category, but I have two examples of women who used flirting as a way to get direct male attention.

Examples of Flirting:

Flirting to achieve a goal

A few years ago I was on a sales call with my sales rep in Dallas. We were in a hospital making a call on the cath lab. Cath labs are pretty busy places and rep heavy, so she and I were waiting our turn to speak to the purchasing guy, Ben. While waiting our turn, a female rep from another company had the floor. She was selling to Ben. She was beautiful. She had long, dark hair, green eyes, and long eyelashes. I won't take that from her . . . but, her approach was awful. I was embarrassed to watch her. It consisted of pleading with Ben, a big teddy bear of a guy, to buy her new product. "Ben, c'mon, pleeeeeease buy it? You know you want to." Ben would resist.

"Aw, Ben." Eyelash batting. "You know if you buy it, I'll buy you lunch." More eyelash batting and hair flipping. "Do this for me, pleeeeease." I literally thought this woman was going to get on her knees, crawl under Ben's desk, and give the guy a blow job. I was just waiting for that. My rep and I kept exchanging looks, full on knowing what she was doing. This was NOT selling. This was begging and using sexuality to get her way. Ben, smart guy, had her figured out and turned her away. I, as a manager at the time, made a mental note to turn her down if her resume ever came across my desk.

Flirting to be fuckable

Okay, I can't claim direct experience with this one, but I can tell you a story that came from a friend of mine who was in a management role with a medical sales company.

She had a female sales rep on her team who was struggling with her sales performance, and had some other issues in the HR area. My friend, the manager, went on some sales calls with her to better evaluate her progress and situation.

On their first sales call of the day, she witnessed her rep speaking to the doctor using baby talk. That's right—baby talk. A grown woman, talking like a little girl. Think Paris Hilton (she was actually criticized for her baby talking, too). Not only did her voice change, but her physical demeanor did as well. She suddenly appeared shy and looked at the doctor through her top lashes. This woman was using this technique to create a level of sexual tension with the physician. My friend said this was such a horribly awkward situation that she could not wait to get out of this doctor's office.

Writing about this makes me cringe. The sales rep was ultimately let go, not because of the baby talking alone, but because of her overall sexualized approach to her relationships with her customers.

Lessons on Flirting:

Flirting is not a healthy way for a woman to set expectations with a customer, colleague, or manager. It is misleading and creates sexual undertones to gain a transaction of some sort. It cheapens you as a woman, and actually discredits the rest of the female population trying to work hard in the right manner.

Rules on Flirting:

1. Do not flirt as a way to gain a transaction.

2. Do not flirt to gain a perceived competitive edge.

3. Do not flirt with the dick clique.

Final Lesson:

Whenever you throw your sexuality out there, the return may not be good. People see through it and will question what you are really made of—this can discredit you as a woman and as a professional. It might help you get a job, deal, or case, but it won't help you keep it. As I mentioned earlier, you are your brand. Do the right things to protect your brand. Your brand will follow you job to job over the lifetime of your career.

8

Testosterone Required

W hile writing this guide, I have done a lot of reflecting. I've thought about what I would do differently. I really wanted to dissect my thoughts, influences, and behaviors. What were my failures or shortcomings? How much of trying to rationalize my challenges is unavoidable estrogen? This has forced me to think of those women who thrive in the dick clique and are mostly unfazed by things I found startling. It was important to me to include this section so that you have an idea of the traits of this type of female in the workplace.

Writing this section prompted me to reach out to a longtime friend and colleague who falls into this much tougher category. Over our years of attending meetings together I had always noticed that she could hang with the guys, drink with the guys, enjoy sports like the guys, but still be this beautiful feminine creature. When we got to speak about this and break down what makes her different, she described it as *boy level*. This is her term, so I can't take credit for it, and she is accurate. The women who thrive and tolerate the dick clique have a higher boy level than most women. What does this mean? This means she engages in male activities flawlessly and tirelessly. And, she is actually interested in male activities. Whether it is sitting out in the freezing cold watching football or hanging out until 3 a.m. in the bar with the guys. Consistently. She could really hold her own, and I think this got her a lot of respect from the dick clique. This is where I struggled, as I do not naturally have such a high boy level as this.

Example of Boy Level:

At a sales meeting a few years ago in Florida, our training sessions had closed and we had some free time before our evening event. The guys wanted to go to the beach to hang out, get some sun, and have a few cocktails. The water was crystal blue, and it was a perfect day, but I chose to go shopping by myself. Thinking nothing of it, I politely declined the beach, grabbed my purse, and headed out to do a little shopping. I'll also tell you that I wanted some downtime. I didn't want to go to the beach to talk shop with the guys. I wanted to clear my head and have some quiet alone time.

My friend, however—the other woman with the high boy level— went with the guys. She threw on her bikini and sunscreen and enjoyed the day with them.

Apparently, this was a fatal flaw for me. This did not do me any favors with the dick clique. Although I had known these guys for years, it didn't look good that I did not join them. She actually approached me about it that night and was rather direct that I should have been there. She said that by not being there, it seemed I did not want to bond with them. I get what she was saying. I get it. In my defense, I really just wanted some quiet time, and, at the same time, nobody needed to see my pasty white shit in a bathing suit. She disagreed with me, and advised that next time I'm presented with a beach opportunity to get over myself, put on a cover-up, and suck it up, buttercup.

Lesson on Boy Level:

My friend was also worried about how her boy level affects other women. She is aware that hers is higher than most. She said she had to raise it at least 15 percent for this job alone, and it was already high before. She said she has always been this type of person. Her worry is that this sets an expectation for other women to be the same, which she knows is not realistic. We talked about the differences between her and me, and acknowledged that she has thicker skin than I do. She said for her survival, she has to be in perfect shape, which she is, be professionally dressed at all times, which she does, and be a completely unflappable bad ass. She does this too, and she does it well. My lesson in all of this as we approach the end of this guide? It's a life cycle. I had already lived the life cycle. My lesson is that each of us will have different ways of handling the dick clique. You will find what works for you. I also know I have ten years on her. There is something to be said for my past experiences, and her arising experiences. She is at the perfect age for taking on the dick clique and knows how to do it skillfully.

Rules on Boy Level:

1. Thicken your skin, whether you plan on increasing your boy level or not. It will help you survive.

2. If your goal is to thrive in the dick clique, up the ante. Do the boy things, but you will have to compromise your girl activities.

3. Know your shit. Meaning, know your business, know your presentations or whatever your career fundamentals require. Don't ever let them see you struggle.

9

Phone a Friend

Find a Female to Confide In

Finding other women to relate to can save your day. I didn't have it for years, and had to keep so much to myself. In the dick clique, there will be times when you feel completely alone, not understanding the environment you are in. This is where having another woman to lean on can be helpful and make you feel normal and grounded. Getting and giving advice as well as just flat-out venting are cathartic and give you sanity when dealing with the dicks.

Examples:

Female Peers

After years of being the only female manager, there was finally another one in another division in the company. I had known her for years and really liked her. What's more, my gut told me I could trust her. She was my saving grace when it came to relating to all of the dick cliquery. We would call each other, share our stories, and just laugh. Not necessarily making fun of our colleagues, but more so at the audacity of comments and actions. One that stands out was a regional conference call with her manager she had called me to tell me about. It was a "rah-rah" call to encourage reps to close more business. On this call he was preaching about never taking no for an answer, to be bullish, fight to get your way, but lastly, not to take shit from operating room directors when it comes to closing business because they are just M.A.B.s. What is an M.A.B., you may ask? Middle. Aged. Bitches. Really. He said this on a conference call. To other women. Dismissing M.A.B.s was part of his sales coaching on that conference call. Wait, I'm in my mid-forties and am female. I guess that makes me an M.A.B., too.

Who else was my colleague to reach out to except me to share this experience? We laughed about it, but not because it was funny. We laughed because we could not believe someone would say that, period. I did my best to support her throughout this phone call because it pissed her off, as it should have. At the same time, I did not want her to feel degraded and I tried to give her encouraging words. Even though she is a tough cookie and is very resilient, I did not want her to feel disrespected or hurt. We had to be there for each other's survival.

Alright, we've gotta talk about HR—the infamous human resources department. You may well know that most HR departments are dominantly made up of women. I have been lucky in that most of the women I have engaged with in HR have been wonderful and turned out to be great friends and guides for me to this day. These relationships can be a positive, and will certainly benefit you in your corporate career, but they come with a certain set of boundaries and rules. As a woman, you still have to be careful when you reach out to HR with an issue. I used HR several times in relevant situations when I really needed their help. I did not use them to play victim, as an outlet to complain, cry, moan, or whine. Use them wisely. If you have an issue you need to discuss, dick clique related or not, think it through and have a solution at hand. Have documentation available to show you have done your homework, and have a plan before you call them. Even though these communications will most likely be woman to woman, you still have to think, function, and execute in a clean, precise, unemotional manner. You need to make sure that HR's perception of you is reputable, knowledgeable, and well planned. The reason is, you will only have so many cards to play in HR when it comes to complaints or confrontations with others. You can't play your whole hand at one time. Use them sparingly and wisely. If you do not, the overuse of HR can be seen as negative and make you seem incapable. I know this sounds awful, but it is true.

My failure is that I didn't use them enough. Even though I had built some solid relationships in HR, I rejected the thought of reaching out to them because I was stubborn when I really should have addressed important issues with them.

Lesson on Female Friends:

Not a lot of lessons here. Just, have them around you. They can be your compass, guide, and companion in all of this dick cliquery.

Rules on Finding a Female Friend:

1. Find a woman you know and trust. This will provide you another layer of security and a safe space to exchange thoughts and issues.

2. Find a friend in HR. From the very beginning. Establish a relationship with her and make sure she knows you. She can be your best ally in difficult situations.

10

Don't Let the Dicks Get You Down

Self-Doubt and Self-Respect

I can't tell you how many situations I have been in where my contributions were overshadowed or ignored by the dick clique. My contributions and input to certain situations were seen as insignificant or flat dumb. If I made a recommendation to my manager or perhaps fellow managers, it would be overshadowed by their "better idea" or they would question if my input was even relevant. This caused me to second-guess myself, beat myself up, and think I wasn't up to par. How were they so much smarter than me? However, I knew in my gut I was on the right track with my input because I had enough life and career experience to know the wiser, but was simply not recognized. If it was not their idea, it was not a good one. The irony is that many of my ideas that were once rejected by the dick clique were ultimately used. Did I get credit? Nope.

Examples:

Self-Doubt

Over my years in medical device sales and management, I have launched new technologies successfully. I've sold them and managed others to do so. I have my own method of planning and execution that proved fruitful and effective. Some years ago we were launching a brand-new technology that was truly innovative and exciting. In our product training, I immediately knew the formula that we would need to launch this new product and I shared my thoughts with the launch team. I was quickly told that my idea would never fly and that we needed to take the direction from the dicks in charge. My ideas got eye rolls, and "pfffft . . . that will never happen" comments. After trying it their way, which felt completely wrong, the new product launch was a disaster. I'll spare you some ugly details like how we were told to just shove product on shelves, but I will tell you it drove a lot of people to quit and they questioned the dicks in charge. After this debacle, I thought, *Fuck it. I'm gonna do it my way.* And guess what? I implemented my strategy, enabled my team to lead, and they did. As a result my team led the company in sales in the following years. I was given very little if any credit for this. If I was acknowledged by the dicks, it was quickly followed by telling me one of the things I had not achieved, and that I'm a terrible manager. My ranking in their world was made clear.

This culture began to break me down. I questioned myself constantly, even though I knew I was engaging in the right activities and coaching the right way. It was a total mind fuck. I felt almost incapacitated knowing that my ideas and contributions were worth nothing to them. Which meant I meant nothing to them. I didn't need this validation for my ego, I just wanted to know that I could trust the people around me and that I had some level of security. When I would ask my male peers about this culture, they shrugged it off and accepted it. They were not treated in the same manner I was. I can tell you this from personal experience. If I did see glimmers of this treatment among the members of the dick clique, it was not as severe and was quickly brushed off by a slap on the back or by having a beer. I knew my rank. I was at the bottom of the food chain. I was told I was weak, and I was perceived as weak. It was like I had lost control of my identity, and it was in the dick clique's hands.

Lessons:

As trite as it sounds, one of my biggest takeaways is to be true to yourself. I knew the best way to approach the launch of the new product, yet I yielded to the dick clique, full on knowing that their strategy would not work. I should have stood up for myself and my beliefs more. I also would not have let their group tank thinking impact my creativity and hinder my success, which I let happen because I kept doubting myself. Ultimately, I started to remove myself from the dick clique members even further. I stopped engaging in their activities, dialogue, and kinship. I now realize the reason I did this is because I did not respect all of the members of the dick clique, and I had a hard time faking it, so I was really withdrawn. This did not do me any favors as I lost a connection with some of my colleagues whom I did like. It was as if I was fading out and my insecurities became a self-fulfilling prophecy.

Rules on Self-Doubt:

1. Stand up for yourself creatively and professionally. If you are faced with adversity in these areas, yet your gut knows better, be brave and stand up.

2. Know your personal limits. If you are at the point of withdrawal, change your attitude, stay engaged, and phone your female friend for support.

3. Don't let them define you. You define you.

Self-Respect

Early on in my career I was spending a day in the field with my sales manager visiting with potential customers and trying to close new business. After a sales call, he and I were in my car on our way to the next call engaging in the ritualistic "How do you think that went?" conversation. During his critique he looked at me and said, "You know, you really need to think like a forty-year-old man." At first, I took this with a grain of salt. I knew I wasn't perfect by any stretch of the imagination, and needed coaching. My second thought as a woman at twenty-four years of age was, *How do I think like a forty-year-old man? Forty is freaking geriatric. Should I be thinking of minivans, comb-overs, and that my wife won't have sex with me anymore?* I gotta tell you, I felt disrespected. As if being a woman would not get me respect? Why did I need to think like a man to be successful? You can act like a woman and be just as successful. I'll never think like a forty-year-old man, nor would I expect any woman to do so.

DON'T LET THE DICKS GET YOU DOWN

Lesson on Self-Respect:

In 2017, I would hope that a male manager would not ask you to think like a man. In 2017, I would hope this conversation would not even take place and that he would give better and more usable advice. Unfortunately, there are those who have not graduated out of the 90s and still think this way. I don't know if there is a solid lesson from my previous example, but it's certainly humorous and drives the point of the dick clique—"Think my way, and you will be fine."

Rules on Self-Respect:

1. If you hear this, "Think like a forty-year-old man," laugh really hard and roll your eyes.

2. If you hear this, ask for better constructive criticism that has nothing to do with gender and will actually help your skills.

3. Stay above it all and respect yourself and your actions.

11

The Good Guys

I have to include this point. Despite all of my dick clique talk, there are good guys and there are plenty of them. I have male friends who became, and still are, my best confidants. I trust these men explicitly These men can strike a balance between the dick clique and normalcy. They know how to play the game, yet come back to reality. There is a difference. I trusted them, relied on them, and they did the same with me. I remember when I won a management award years ago, and I had to get up and give a speech in front of our whole sales force. I vigorously thanked my sales team, and then thanked my all-male management colleagues by stating that I felt they were "brothers from another mother." The crowd laughed. I didn't expect that because I didn't think it was funny. Their response made me feel vulnerable and maybe even a little embarrassed. I wanted the crowd to take me seriously—what I was expressing was honest and heartfelt, and wasn't funny to me. I got over that moment of misunderstanding and moved on. However, to this day I really adore those "brothers." They helped me survive the dick clique.

12

Did I Survive?

So here is the question. Did I survive the dick clique? Dammit, I did. It came with failures, regrets, successes, happiness, and conflict. Surviving the dick clique has given me inner peace, knowledge, maturity, and foresight. It has taught me to function with clarity and has given me a purpose—that purpose is bigger than what I experienced and can be helpful to you. It is to give you a path and guide for your coming years as a professional woman. I want to see each of you work with dignity, respect, and to lead by example. Know your worth and believe in yourself. I also want you to see humor in your experiences and know that mistakes are normal and healthy.

You may be asking, "Alright, now we know what happens in the dick clique. How do we change it?" I do not have all of the answers to this one very important question. I wish I did. I am no expert, but will certainly give you my thoughts.

Firstly, my ideas are purely what I think we can do on a ground roots level. What I do firmly believe is that this starts with us and it starts at home as parents with children. We need to encourage our daughters to excel in their life ventures, teach them there are no boundaries, and inspire and encourage them to be leaders. As for our sons, do the same, but also teach them that women are equals and that women need to be respected. Actually, way before I had experienced the dick clique, I had always promised myself that if I was ever lucky enough to have a son that I would do this. I think that by encouraging and creating new behaviors we will change the culture and create a healthier space for men and women to work side by side.

Secondly, surprisingly I have had some men reach out to me knowing this book would soon be released. I think the topic of *surviving the dick clique* kind of threw them at first. The response I got from them was, "I didn't know I was doing this. What can I do differently?" Let me tell you, I was happy to hear these words. It was enlightening and refreshing. It was a sign that we can change and that we have willing parties to do so. It gave me hope and made my heart feel lighter. This inspired me more to think about ways to make things better—and that just by increasing awareness we can make a start. Laughingly, this created awareness for me. I'd rather us find solutions together and have it be a collaborative effort. This will give us the power to change.

Until we reach that place where men and women truly work as equals side by side . . . Ladies, here is your guide. Here are your rules.[1]

---

[1]   Join us at www.dickclique.com to share your stories and ideas about how we can reach that much needed work environment—a place for true collaboration, devoid of exclusions of all kinds.